"INSIDERS GUIDE" TO GETTING A JOB IN PHARMACEUTICAL SALES

BECOME A PHARMACEUTICAL SALES REPRESENTATIVE

Inside Tips from One Who Has Real-life Experience in Pharmaceutical Sales

EARNING POTENTIAL UP TO $100,000

COMPENSATION PACKAGE INCLUDES

SALARY, BONUS, COMPANY CAR....AND

MORE!

1

- Be part of the healthcare industry
  - Help people
  - Make a great living
  - Work from home

READ ABOUT HOW MY REAL-LIFE
EXPERIENCE CAN HELP
YOU
ACHIEVE YOUR GOAL OF MOVING INTO
PHARMACEUTICAL SALES

DR. CHARLES O. DARAMOLA

TABLE OF CONTENTS

6. Getting Your Resume in Front of Potential Employers

INSIDER TIP #4

7. A "Must Have" for Your Interview

INSIDER TIP #5

8. Remember the Acronym OATO during Your Interview

INSIDER TIP #6

9. You Are Hired!

10. How to Get a 10% Raise in One Year

INSIDER TIP #7

A FINAL WORD OF WISDOM AND HOW TO CONTACT ME FOR CONSULTATION!

CHAPTER 1

YOU CAN MAKE A GREAT LIVING IN
PHARMACEUTICAL SALES

Congratulations! You are taking a significant step towards securing a well-paying job in pharmaceutical sales. If you don't know by now, let me assure you that many positions in pharmaceutical sales pay extremely well. Although starting salaries vary, pharmaceutical sales representatives can obtain a compensation package worth $50,000+ in their very first year! Top-notch and experienced pharmaceutical sales representatives can earn up to and over $100,000 in total compensation, and most jobs include a base salary, company car, and the opportunity to make substantial income in bonuses.

In short, when you consider the complete compensation package and other financial incentives that are available, you have the potential to help people with different illnesses and make very good living.

Before we go any further, I would like to make a few things clear. The contents of this book are MY experience and mine only. I am not reflecting the views of any particular pharmaceutical company or the pharmaceutical industry. The "insider information" has nothing to do with the "insider trading" we sometimes hear about on Wall Street.

I am not privy to any special information that would help me make money on Wall Street. My insider information is based on my experience on how I got my jobs in pharmaceutical sales and that is what I am sharing with you. I want to use MY experience to help YOU. This is MY story. Let's get started!

The world of pharmaceutical sales can be amazing because you will be **helping people** who face a multitude of diseases live healthier lives. You will be promoting or "detailing" (as it is often described in the industry) drugs to physicians—drugs which will be used to treat diseases ranging from high blood pressure to depression and cancer. Many of the drugs will not only enhance the lives of patients, but may also save their lives. Imagine the satisfaction you will feel in helping individuals and their families improve their quality of life, while you are also supporting yourself and your family with a valuable career.

To keep updated on the marketplace, I recently conducted an online search for pharmaceutical and biotech sales openings on a few job websites. The search resulted in nearly 30 pages and about 2,000 job openings! The jobs themselves ranged from entry-level to more experienced sales jobs, manager jobs, trainer jobs, and everything in-between. Many of the sales jobs offered a guaranteed salary, bonuses for outstanding results, use of a company car, and other financial incentives. All of these promising job opportunities are available for those with determination and persistence.

If you are reading this book, you are probably such an individual; you want to help people, you want to take care of your family, and you are willing to pursue your goals. A pharmaceutical sales job may be your ticket to accomplishing all of these goals—and many others.

YOU too can have a great career in pharmaceutical sales, just as I did. As a Specialty Sales Representative for major pharmaceutical companies, I made a good living (I can share specific compensation numbers with you if you email me at Consultpharma1@gmail.com). Let me clarify one important point: **I cannot guarantee how well you will do as a pharmaceutical sales representative. YOU determine you own success.** Perhaps as the saying goes "death and taxes" are probably the only guarantees one can be certain of in life! With that said, I am living proof that great goals are within one's reach. With experience, hard work, a positive attitude and dedication, you can do as well or even better than I have done. I was very good at my job and worked very hard to reach lofty goals. I provided physicians with on-label clinical data and discussed the benefits and side effects of my promoted products. You too can do the same in order to earn a great salary, work for great companies, provide life-enhancing drugs for sick people, and make a good living for you and your family.

But let us not skip ahead of ourselves. First, you have to GET a job in pharmaceutical sales.

Remember you are the only one who can get the well-paying job you want and deserve. Your skills, your background, your experience and determination will move you forward to your goals. **Getting the job will be your job!** And my **Insiders Guide** will point you in the right direction.

This guide will provide you with insider tips, resume tips, pre- and post-interview tips, buzz words, and suggestions on "do's and don'ts" from an "insider" who has worked in the pharmaceutical industry for over a decade.

CHAPTER 2

WHY MY "INSIDER INFORMATION" IS SO UNIQUE

You may be asking yourself: how can this book help me? What kind of knowledge and "insider information" does the writer of this book really possess?

I call myself an "insider" because I have worked in the pharmaceutical industry for well over 10 years, and most of those years were in pharmaceutical sales. Some of my job titles included: Primary Care Pharmaceutical Sales Representative, Specialty Care Pharmaceutical Sales Representative (including respiratory, cardiovascular, neuroscience specialties) and also as a Market Development Representative. I moved through the ranks to an Assistant Director position. I have worked for a few pharmaceutical companies, been through dozens of successful interviews, was continually hired, and managed to negotiate great terms each time. The companies I worked for were not desperate for "bodies." They were in fact major companies ranking in the top 20 international pharmaceutical companies looking for the "cream of the crop."

The "insider tips" I offer you in this book will **DEFINITELY SET YOU APART** from other potential job candidates. My information is based on many years of successful experience.

I KNOW how to find and obtain high-paying jobs in pharmaceuticals. My **Insiders Guide** is not based on research that others have done, nor is it based on "he said she said," as some other authors might do. While other guides might seem similar to mine, many of the authors did not actually draw on first-hand experience of what it takes to find and keep a high-paying sales job in the industry. Instead, they interviewed "experts" (usually someone like me with first-hand experience), summarized the input provided by the "expert," and sell the information to you. Well, you can do the same—just interview a few people in the industry, pick their brains for the same information, and write your own guide. On the other hand, nothing is more valuable than the first-hand knowledge and experience of someone who has been through the field from beginning to end and will share that knowledge and experience with you in a systematic, step-by-step way. I know first-hand what leads to success and what doesn't because I have "been there, done that."

I have found what works best, and I know it can work for you.

CHAPTER 3

THE EDUCATIONAL BACKGROUND THAT DRUG COMPANIES WANT

The level of education that pharmaceutical companies seek varies from company to company. Let's explore this area of educational background a little bit more.

The majority of pharmaceutical companies require the minimum of a Bachelor's degree. However, there are still many opportunities even if you have less than a Bachelor's. Pharmaceutical companies want to see stellar credentials, a proven track record of achievement, strong sales experience, and the ability to grasp scientific knowledge. If a hiring manager believes you have what it takes, you have as good a chance as anybody else even without the minimum educational requirement.

So whatever your educational background, put your best foot forward and let the chips fall accordingly. A college degree may (I stress **may**) give you a slight advantage, but how you present your resume **and yourself** during the interview will likely be the deciding factors that will get you the job.

Like most other industries, pharmaceutical companies examine everything you bring to the table. Some companies will at least be willing to grant you an interview if you have an Associate's degree, while others may insist on a Bachelor's degree. Some companies may opt to place more weight on your experience and proven record of success.

Keep this in mind: My experience assures me that most companies evaluate you on the "complete package": which includes education, along with experience, personality, manner of presentation, and so on. The practice of pharmaceutical companies is probably no different from any industry. While a Bachelor's definitely helps, it is usually not the deal-breaker with all companies. What matters most is to obtain the interview and place your foot squarely in the door. Sealing the deal will be based on who you are, what you bring to the table, and what you feel you can offer the prospective company.

For this reason, your experience and qualifications, and how you lay these out in your resume, are so important.

There are no hard and fast rules when it comes to a college major or specialization. The top pharmaceutical companies have been known to hire candidates with majors in business, biology, liberal arts and the sciences—almost anything that a college can offer. What seems to be the "bottom line" is that equally important as the degree is the type of experience candidates possess and communicate to their prospective employer.

INSIDER TIP #1

Most pharmaceutical companies require a Bachelor's degree, but some do not. There are usually no hard and fast rules about college majors, but <u>*not*</u> *having a college degree is usually not a deal-breaker.*

CHAPTER 4

THE EXPERIENCE THAT

PHARMACEUTICAL COMPANIES LIKE TO SEE

If you are new to the industry, don't despair! Pharmaceutical companies prefer, but do not require pharmaceutical sales experience.

Many of the major pharmaceutical companies do look for sales experience, but the level and type of experience can vary. Some sales representatives have entered the industry with experiences including copier sales experience, business-to-business sales, and consumer sales. Even so, sales experience is not a strict requirement.

When I started in pharmaceutical sales many years ago, I had no pharmaceutical sales experience per se and came from a consumer sales background, yet I was immediately hired at a very lucrative salary plus bonus, plus a company car.

It is important to remember that people from all backgrounds; such as computer sales, retail sales, teachers, people with backgrounds in communication and fresh college graduates—can be hired into pharmaceutical sales. The key point to keep in mind is that you always have a chance even if your background is not in sales or pharmaceuticals, because the key is how you present yourself and your experience and show that you have the ability to sell.

I know of a young man who was hired as a pharmaceutical sales representative, even though his experience was limited to retail sales. However, he had a wonderful personality which persuaded the company to hire him, and he subsequently did very well in pharmaceutical sales. Some people can be hired right out of college with very little work experience because they have many other qualities to sell their potential. Pharmaceutical companies have well staffed training departments and will put you through a very rigorous regimen of Anatomy and Physiology, Pharmacology, Effective Selling and other courses that will give you a strong clinical and sales foundation.

INSIDER TIP #2

Prior pharmaceutical experience is not required to be hired for an entry-level job in pharmaceutical sales.

After a couple of years in an entry-level sales position "calling" on primary care physicians, you may seek a promotion into Specialty Sales. This is a more specialized position with much more clinical selling—calling on specialists such as Cardiologists, Neurologists, and Psychiatrists. To enter Specialty Sales, candidates usually need a few years of successful pharmaceutical sales experience. Two to three years of successful primary care sales experience is good enough to help you move into Specialty Sales, either with your current company or with a new company. At that point, you can begin to increase your earning potential substantially!

First things first. Regardless of the kind of work experience you have, you must present yourself as a professional with people skills, flexibility, confidence, and self-motivation. With such assets, you will undoubtedly do well in anything you set out to accomplish, including finding a satisfying job and succeeding in pharmaceutical sales. If you do not have some of these skills, and you are currently employed, try to accumulate some on-the-job training in public speaking and communications. If you are not currently employed, some profit and not-for-profit organizations can help you with public speaking and communications. I have a few suggestions; just contact me at: consultpharma1@gmail.com

A popular motivational saying—which you may have seen on bumper stickers—goes something like this: shoot for the moon…but if you miss, land among the stars. But I prefer a twist on this: Never shoot for the moon; always aim for the stars, and if you miss, you might just land on the moon. After all, if you only have your eye on the moon, you may miss and fall back to earth with a resounding thud. I think this is a good practical approach to follow in a world with no

guarantees but lots of promises.

CHAPTER 5

IMPRESS PHARMECEUTICAL COMPANIES BY INCLUDING "THIS" ON YOUR RESUME

No matter how impressive your background may be, if you do not convey your "impressiveness" on your resume, you reduce your chances of even cinching an interview. So you must display your resume in the strongest way possible to give yourself a shot at an interview. Truthfully and assertively emphasize your strong points to impress pharmaceutical companies and potential employers that you have what it takes to be a successful sales representative. Never be dishonest on your resume by stretching, inflating, embellishing or exaggerating your reality.

BUT DON'T UNDERSELL YOURSELF EITHER. Include your strengths and achievements with pride and assurance. Here are a few very important resume tips.

Always try quantifying your successes by adding numbers/figures to your achievements. For example:

➢ Instead of saying "increased business," be more specific by saying, **"increased business by 20%."**

➢ Instead of saying "recognized as an outstanding student," rank your achievements as follows: **"ranked #1 out of 100 students' in my graduating class."**

➢ Instead of saying "increased productivity," quantify your achievements by stating, **"reduced manufacturing lead-time by 10%."**

I cannot stress enough the need to rank/quantify your achievements accurately. Be honest and have the necessary documentation to back your claims. In any of your past experiences, whether as a student, teacher or police officer, always rank your achievements in factual ways. Pharmaceutical companies love rankings. Sales representatives and managers are ranked all the time, so quantifying your achievements will make your credentials more impressive to hiring managers.

INSIDER TIP #3

Always rank and quantify achievements.

In addition, as is recommended for any resume, include action words such as **achieved, established, started, doubled, ranked**, and so on. Pharmaceutical companies like to see that you are action-oriented. Be proactive, not reactive.

Another point for resumes is to list and discuss major educational and career achievements. All your successes, accomplishments, important and relevant career milestones should be included on your resume. In addition, you should have a mental inventory of any action in your career and in your personal life that demonstrate you are a go-getter, not a quitter—a person who can overcome adversity. You should be able to articulate both in writing and verbalize these admirable traits and experiences to potential employers.

CHAPTER 6

GETTING YOUR RESUME IN FRONT OF

POTENTIAL EMPLOYERS

I will not spend a lot of time on what every job hunter has inevitably come to know by now—the importance of **utilizing social media**. My **Insiders Guide** is meant to provide you with information you may not necessarily know unless you are already in the pharmaceutical industry. With that said, I hope you already have a presence on Linkedin and Facebook. If not, join the networks as early in your job-searching career as possible.

One of our modern realities is that potential employers and recruiters may do a background check on you by researching and scanning through social networking sites. Make sure your "Linkedin" profile is up to date; eliminate all unprofessional information or messages from your social network profile and other sites that will detract from your potential marketability. You may think that only your friends will see your comments, but your "Wall" might be open to a wider audience. Like it or not, unprofessional comments and postings may influence others (potential employers) adversely and convey the wrong impression about you. Potential employers may assume that if you use bad judgment on "Facebook" you may also do so in the work place—and this is hardly the message you want to give prospective employers, even before you set foot in their office.

Networking (with a Twist)

I am sure you have heard that "networking" is a key component of any job search. You might have been asked to call your employed friends for tips and leads about possible job openings, or you have been told to attend networking events and gatherings to get introductions and uncover leads. It is important to continue doing those things, of course, but I also want to share with you a few networking sources that are too frequently overlooked when trying to find a job in pharmaceutical sales.

Your family physician

Your personal, family or neighborhood physician may be your **secret networking weapon** as you embark on your journey to a career in pharmaceutical sales. Why? Physicians are the primary target audience for pharmaceutical sales representatives. The job of a pharmaceutical sales representative involves visiting physicians to provide them with drug and disease information and share the features, benefits and side effects of drug treatments for different diseases. A key part of this process is getting to know physicians and their staff, gaining access to their practice, and building relationships with them. If you already have a good and comfortable relationship with your own family physician, you may let him or her know that you are seeking a job in pharmaceutical sales and ask if he or she might be willing to introduce you to pharmaceutical representatives who call on the practice. Of course, neither the physician nor the pharmaceutical sales representative is obligated to do anything for you. Promising to do anything that seems to be trading favors is illegal. But nothing prohibits the doctor from introducing you to the representative, or giving you the representative's business card and then you can contact the sales representative yourself.

You could pursue this in a number of ways. Office managers, administrative staff and physicians usually have business cards for different sales representatives on file; you could ask for their contact information and call the representatives' directly. You could enlist the help of the doctor by asking him or her to inquire from visiting pharmaceutical representatives which companies are hiring or expanding. Both methods can work and can be the first step in getting your resume into the hands of a current pharmaceutical employee. Alternatively, you could ask your doctor for business cards from specific sales representatives from companies that interest you, and contact the specific sales representatives. The sales representative may be willing to pass your resume on to the appropriate people in the company.

Your local pharmacist

Your local pharmacist may also be a good source of information on how to obtain a job in pharmaceutical sales. In addition to calling on physicians' offices, many sales representatives also visit pharmacies and have good rapport with pharmacists.

Your pharmacist is an expert on drugs and is knowledgeable about disease states as well as the manufacturers of relevant drugs. They may also be able to provide you with the business cards of sales representatives which they often keep on file, along with information on who manufactures which drugs.

INSIDER TIP #4

Use your local physician, family doctor and the local pharmacist as valuable networking resources.

Internet/Company websites/Classifieds

One way to begin a fruitful job search is to go on the Internet and browse the various websites of the pharmaceutical companies. All major companies have their own website with a list of available job opportunities, along with directions on how you can apply for the positions. If you are not sure of which specific company interests you, use any of the search engines and type in "pharmaceutical companies" to begin introducing yourself to the field.

You could also search through online career services such as careerbuilder.com, monster.com, hotjobs.com, among others, under specific sales categories such as pharmaceutical, biotechnology and medical sales. Another strategy is to comb through the classified newspapers in your area. Look in the sales career section of the Classifieds, especially in the local Sunday editions which often devote an entire section to employment.

Although you may want to peruse the whole career opportunities section, pay close attention to the SALES section, which is where most pharmaceutical sales jobs will be listed.

Recruiters

Another popular and successful route to a new job is by contacting recruiters who specialize in the pharmaceutical industry. Again, a search on the Internet for "pharmaceutical recruiters" can lead you to a number of possibilities. Check also in the classified employment section of your local newspaper, usually under "employment agencies" or "recruiters." The titles for sales jobs in the classifieds of your local paper or in your web search will vary by source, but will typically contain the words such as: Employment Agency Sales, Pharmaceutical Sales Biotech Sales or Medical Sales You will usually be asked to email or fax your resume and you will then be contacted for an interview if the company feels they can use your skills. You can contact me if you need additional guidance including resume help, interview tips or any other related subjects; email me at: consultpharma1@gmail.com

Even if a recruiting agency responds saying they cannot help you, do not hesitate to ask for their advice on preparing yourself for the pharmaceutical industry—how to make your candidacy stronger, what work experience is needed on your resume, and so on. Recruiters can often provide some very helpful advice for you in pursuing future prospects.

CHAPTER 7

A "MUST HAVE" FOR YOUR INTERVIEW

It won't be necessary for me to review in depth "the basics" on how to prepare for your interviews - researching the targeted company, understanding the company's mission, arriving punctually for your appointments, speaking clearly, exuding confidence, and so on. Such practical information is available on numerous websites and in many guide books for job-seeking in today's world. Instead, as I stressed earlier, my goal is to provide you with some **INSIDER TIPS** that are specific to pharmaceutical sales. Let's consider some of these unique aspects of interviewing with pharmaceutical companies.

Phone interview with human resources

Often many companies will begin with a phone interview conducted by someone from human resources, whose job is to screen in/out potential candidates. Usually human resources personnel will have reviewed your resume with a fine-toothed comb, thus it is vital that you know the details on your own resume inside out. Before the interview, practice describing the contents of your resume to someone else who can help you identify weak spots or point out something you have overlooked. Many consulting services can also help you with your resume and prep you for your interview. You can also contact me for help at consultpharma1@gmail.com

If you do well on the phone interview, the next step will usually be a face-to-face interview with a hiring manager. **At the end of the human resources phone interview, it does not hurt to ask the**

interviewer for feedback and request advice on areas he or she thinks need improvement. I once asked my phone interviewer for some feedback and he was kind enough to share some of the strengths as well as the flaws he saw in my resume. As a result, I made the changes, received an in-person interview, and was accepted for the job! Of course not all HR employees will be so helpful, but it is always worth a try.

A "MUST HAVE" for your interview

One responsibility you will have as a pharmaceutical sales representative is what I call "show and tell." You will be "selling" and promoting your products by showing and sharing with numerous physicians the sales and promotional pieces that your company has developed and that have been approved by the Food and Drug Administration. Because pharmaceutical companies are keen on "show and tell," it would be extremely helpful for your interview to assemble an actual "show and tell brag book" of your prior experiences and achievements. That is, literally putting together a three-hole binder or portfolio case that collects all your awards, certificates, letters of commendation and other documentation that can testify to your achievements.

The industry often refers to this type of display as a "brag book" which, in a sense, is a book "bragging" about your achievements. While you may at first think you do not have anything or much to include in a "brag book," think about your prior job evaluations and commendations—no matter how small they seem—and copy them to insert in your brag book. If you are fresh out of college, you may want to include a summary research paper that you are particularly proud of and talk about it during the interview. Similarly, you could pick a project from one of your jobs or from college that you deem to be exceptional work, and copy that for your brag book to discuss during the interview. When you really think deeply about what you have accomplished even in what seems a limited time span or arena, I am sure you can discover things you have done that are worthy of praise that will make important contributions for a "brag book."

INSIDER TIP #5

Set yourself apart by putting together a "brag book" and share it during your interview.

Preparing for the interview—"Role Play"

I mentioned earlier about involving your local physician or family doctor as resources in your process of job-seeking. Ask your family physician or any physician you know and are comfortable with if you can sit in on a "detail" - the industry term for a sales presentation from one of his/her pharmaceutical sales representatives. Sitting in and observing the presentation will give you a clearer idea of what a sales representative does for a living. It may also give you the opportunity to speak to and "pick the brain" of the sales representative right on the spot. Moreover, witnessing firsthand what a "pharmaceutical detail" looks like, will prepare you to give a "detail" during your interview with more authority and confidence. These are all things I can help you with as well. For a reasonable fee, I can help you with "detail" or "role play" practice.

In addition, practice selling an item to a friend—a watch, a pen—or better yet, select a product from your medicine cabinet at home—cough mixture, aspirin, mouthwash—and practice selling its features and benefits to your "potential customer." (Of course, be sure to do your "homework" by understanding the product as much as possible) Ask your friend to voice as many objections (i.e., reasons NOT to buy) as possible and then find ways to combat these objections. This is called "role play" in pharmaceutical sales. When you get hired, you will be doing a lot of role plays. Become comfortable using open-ended questions that do not have "yes" or "no" answers. By role playing, you are in fact prepping for your interview. The interviewer will want to gauge your selling skills, see how you perform under pressure, and will likely simulate a selling situation. The practice sessions I am recommending will be very helpful for this purpose. Contact me if you need help prepping. Email: consultpharma1@gmail.com

CHAPTER 8

REMEMBER THE ACRONYM "OATO"

DURING YOUR INTERVIEW

Of course, you know the basics—dress appropriately, arrive on time, make eye contact, and so on—that will be the same for every interview. But a key element for pharmaceutical industry interviews is giving examples of how you have handled difficult situations in the past. You should be prepared discuss situations where you were confronted with a problem, resolved it, and produced a (hopefully) positive outcome because of your action.

I have coined the acronym **OATO** to help you remember this key element for your interview:

➤ What was the **O**BSTACLE you encountered?

➤ What **A**CTION did you take?

➤ What was the **T**HINKING driving your action?

➤ What was the final **O**UTCOME of your action?

INSIDER TIP #6

Remember the acronym OATO for your interview.

Use OATO to strengthen your interview, but of course, always frame your interview in the basics as you would in any other interview: be prepared and professional, know what your prospective company is about, speak clearly, with conviction, look directly into the interviewer's eyes, and convey with confidence that what you can bring to the table will help the company achieve its goals. Talk less about what you

want and more how you can fulfill what **THEY** want.

Bottom line: How will be organization be better off by

hiring **YOU?**

CHAPTER 9

YOU ARE HIRED!

If you follow all of the practical advice and insider tips I have offered in this book, you stand a good chance of landing a job that will be a great match for you and the company. You will see how all your preparation and effort for the interview will pay off in obtaining a job that is both challenging and extremely satisfying. You will finally have the rewarding responsibility of helping doctors help their patients improve their quality of life. You will also see the possibilities ahead of you of being successful, building a strong portfolio, and ensuring that your entry in the pharmaceutical industry is perhaps just the first step towards a lifelong career.

Because I been in this industry for years as well as speaking with many people outside the industry, I know that a common misperception is that selling pharmaceuticals is an easy job. I can assure you it is not. Your first six months will likely be the most challenging, especially in becoming accustomed to the company, the volume of work you are given, the amount of studying and training. You will also be required to take knowledge based examinations in order to be able to discuss your products intelligently. Accept guidance and feedback from your manager, more experienced coworkers, mentors and trusted advisors. Pace yourself and draw on your innate determination, your personality, your "never quit" attitude (which helped to get you the job in the first place!) and you should succeed and gradually move up the ranks in the industry.

Do not hesitate to ask the inevitable questions that occur to all new employees learning a new job. If you are unsure of certain "rules of the game" or how to do certain parts of your job...ASK FOR HELP! You will find that most pharmaceutical companies have excellent training departments and the trainers will shepherd you through initial sales training with great expertise. Your manager and other team members will also prove to be good resources. You can also contact me for advice at consultpharma1@gmail.com

CHAPTER 10

HOW TO GET A 10% RAISE IN ONE YEAR!

You know the drill: at the end of the year if you are lucky, you will get a "raise." In a good year, it might be 3-5%, but more likely in the 2-3% range. So with some hypothetical calculation, if you are making $40,000, a 3% raise will be $1,200 per year or an average of $200 dollars a month.

That said, there **is** a way to get a 10% raise in one year! Drug companies are very competitive and would not hesitate to recruit you away from your present company if they feel you would be a valuable addition to their team. They would then be willing to **pay** you to join their team. Once you get your dream sales job, your goal should be to grow sales of the product you promote in your territory and possibly become the market leader or at a minimum show consistent and impressive sales growth. As a result, if you can garner a few awards from your present company like "Representative of the Year" or become a member of the "President's Club" (these are awards given for outstanding sales results) display leadership skills and show consistent growth for at least two years, then recruiters have a way of hearing about you and an opportunity may present itself where you can join another company with a much higher salary.

Even if you are not contacted by recruiters, proactively send your resume to other companies and pharmaceutical sales recruiters documenting your successes and achievements. Companies will reward you handsomely if they know you can help their organization and offer you financial incentives to lure you away— potentially with a 10-15% increase over your current salary in some cases. I did it early in my career was able to increase my income much more quickly than if I had stayed with same company. Of course, there are drawbacks to moving around—you will lose seniority, longevity in one company, vacation hours, and so on. But only you can determine what is best for you and your situation. After you have been in the industry a few years, you can decide what you need to do next to keep growing and continue feeling satisfied in your work.

INSIDER TIP #7

Get a big raise by cashing in on your success.

A FINAL WORD OF WISDOM

Although my book has mainly discussed how to get a good job in pharmaceutical sales, it is also important to keep in mind that you will be promoting life-enhancing and life-saving medications to physicians. Remember that you will be doing honorable work, despite the often negative comments you might hear from the media about the "greedy" pharmaceutical companies.

You need to face the reality that some people and/or situations will give the drug companies a bad name. There are individuals within the industry who have forgotten that the real reason for drugs is to help those who are sick, and it is possible for you to make a good living while promoting those drugs to the medical profession. Those who think it is only about sales and making money do a great disservice to the industry and all its benefits. The reality is that you may encounter other sales representatives who are driven only by monetary gain. You may also learn about companies with cultures that focus only on sales, market share, and dollars as the be-all and end-all.

My advice to you is the following: if you ever feel uncomfortable with what you are doing, if the vibes you get from the company you work trouble you, and if your internal moral compass is telling you that "business as usual" does not feel right, then make plans to switch careers or move to another company with a culture that feels right for you.

DO NOT STAY JUST FOR THE MONEY!

If you have to, find another line of work, go back to school, get additional training and develop a different skill set. The longer you stay in the pharmaceutical industry, the more difficult it will be to remove yourself from it.

On the other hand, if you feel good about what you are doing, if you feel the corporate culture of your organization is ethical and above board and in-line with your "world view" then enjoy yourself because you **are** helping many more people than you realize while also making a good living.

GOOD LUCK!

The insider information I have provided will not guarantee you a job, but the insider tips can increase your chances of finding a good job. I am sure many of you still have questions that were not answered in this book. There are additional sources can be used to supplement this Insider Guide. The Internet is replete with resources that can help you in your job search. Do your homework, surf the Web looking for job guides, interview guides, and so on. If you need your resume reviewed, interview coaching, buzzword coaching, or additional advice on getting a job in the pharmaceutical industry in sales, there are a number of recruiting agencies or "head hunters" that specialize in the pharmaceutical industry. Use this guide as a springboard, then research and utilize additional resources. If anything, this guide hopes you will discover the potential, promise, and confidence you innately possess to succeed in your job search. I will be providing fee based consulting for those of you who may want one on one individualized coaching or additional "insider tips".

Just contact at: consultpharma1@gmail.com

I wish you the best of luck!

Dr. Charles O. Daramola

www.ingramcontent.com/pod-product-compliance
Lightning Source LLC
Chambersburg PA
CBHW071633170526

45166CB00003B/1317